Soulful Pourings:

Poems and Prompts for Growth and Healing

Written by

Patrice Sheri

Key2Life Publishing

Waldorf, Maryland

Written by Patrice Sheri

Published by Key2Life Publishing

Waldorf, Maryland

ISBN: 979-8-9924471-2-5

Printed in the United States of America

Acknowledgements

To my **grandmothers** who taught me how to **serve**.

To my **mother** who taught me how to **love**.

To my **God**, who taught me how to release what no longer **serves** or **loves**.

To my **sister**, who set the example for **academic success**.

To my **husband**, who exposed me to paths of **finding God** for myself and the boldness to **speak the truth** regardless of the circumstances.

To my three sons, who sing a **psalm** of **purpose, serenity, abundance, love and mercy which makes life liveable.**

To my special friend, whom I lost to breast cancer, who taught me the true meaning of **forgiveness.**

And to the authentic friends, who **know my story,** possessed **staying power,** modeled **true friendship, celebrated me** in good times and bad, and had the **courage** to tell me the truth when I did not want to hear it, and who made it easy to **reciprocate** those same sentiments to others.

Foreword

Welcome to the enchanting world of "Soulful Pourings," where every line, every verse, whispers secrets of the soul and echoes the profound depths of human experience. Within these pages lies not just a collection of poems, but a sanctuary where vulnerability dances hand in hand with resilience, where the raw essence of the human spirit finds its voice.

Prepare to embark on a journey unlike any other—a journey that will not only touch your heart but ignite the very essence of your being. As you turn the pages of this soul-stirring book, you will find yourself immersed in a tapestry of emotions, where tears flow freely, laughter echoes joyously, and every word resonates with the symphony of life.

Through Patrice's poignant narratives and evocative verse, you will witness the beauty of imperfection, the strength found in vulnerability, and the power of connection that binds us all. Each poem is a testament to the resilience of the human spirit, a reminder that even in our darkest moments, there is light to be found.

So, dear sister, open your heart wide and allow yourself to be swept away by the sheer beauty and wisdom that grace these pages. Let the words of "Soulful Pourings" wrap around you like a warm embrace, offering solace, empathy, and a profound sense of kinship. For within these lines, you will find not only poetry but the essence of what it means to be human and flawed.

-Traci Wynn

At an early age, she knew..

I look in her eyes and it is as if she sees her future and contemplates on whether she should even travel the path that has been ordained for her.

One cheek filled with a lemon, the other with an orange.

There is an energy of indifference in her smirky smile. Knowing all will begin with the sour taste of a lemon but end with the pleasure, joy and sweetness in an orange.

The lemon phases will build her confidence through anger, resentment, and the stream of disappointments.

But the puckering of her lips are able to fully and completely appreciate the sweetness of the orange.

A taste of sweetness that comes with sunshine dreams that light up the world, regardless of time zone, savoring her commitment and service to others.

The path thick, and bumpy like the skin of the fruit where the lemon cleanses and clears the path to see a bold, bright orange scented with abundance clinging to cloves, aged with the dreams that would come true.

At an early age, she knew...
The lemons would paralyze her.

The astringent would be too strong for her sensitive nature, causing her skin to react and become a human art show of internal struggles being viewed externally.
Critiqued.
Defined.
Questioned.
Labeled hypersensitive.

The orange would mobilize her.
Give her the creativity to sit down and write these pourings of expressed emotions.
Freedom.
Passion.
Intuition.
Emotionally balanced.

The citrus genus
Climbing the status of the family ranking which shifts the lineage toward
Peace, prosperity and ease.
Pouring the juices of both fruits, the lemon and the orange.
Achieving intergenerational healing.
A filled cup, raised high, as libation to the ancestors.
Poured out of respect and homage to heal the
Familial line and the land.
With love.

About Soulful Pourings

These writings are mere pourings from my soul. Some stem from personal experiences, while others from the empathic telepathy found in the spirits of other souls. The purpose of writing is for the reader to find or connect with those that resonate with them. Identify why it resonates and to write a response to the pourings that may help another to change their perspective, rewrite their stories from a compassionate lens. It is meant to be interactive, a giving and receiving experience that will hold space for those in our community and help us learn to remember to be of service to others.

Table of Contents

Acknowledgements iii
Foreword iv
At an early age, she knew v
About Soulful Pourings vii
Table of Contents viii

Section 1 .... **11**

The Elements, Fire Prevails 12
Pride 14
Fragile 17
A Change in My Story 18
Sterling Silver 20
Oasis 21
A New Year 22
Live Longer, See Clearer 23
Female Porcupine 24
The Winnings 26
Words Are Your Jam 27
tWitch 29
Focus on the We, Not the They 31
Burdens Are Not Meant for You to Bear 33
The Medicine 35
Zion 37
Colored Purple 39
Releasing the Timid Spirit 41

Section 2 .... **43**

Loving with Gratitude 44
Distance 45
YOU 47

She is 48

Grandfather...49

The Rib Cage 50

Worst Friend 52

Catharsis 53

Fear of Rejection 54

A True Friend 56

Training Our Children 58

God's Goddess... 60

Section 3 .... **63**

A Revelation..64

Only When I am Ready To Read 66

Crash 68

Prayer, Where are you?................................69

The Cycle of Friendship 70

Our Prayer..72

The Leprechaun: God & Time.....................74

Rest..76

Peace in Overflow.......................................77

Know the Plans 78

Pleasing Faith... 80

Renewed Strength 81

Bravery, Courage Within You 83

A Divine Invitation.....................................85

Thirst Calling 87

Casting Call 89

The Journey to Find a Place 90

Patience with Power-Filled Process.............91

x

Section 1

A Journey of Self: Finding Strength, Identity, and Purpose

This section explores the self as a central point of experience, how we are shaped by challenges, how we find our identity, and how we learn to love and accept ourselves.

The Elements, Fire Prevails

The air I breathe, love.

The earth I inhabit, living.

The tears I cry when I love and live, water.

The hurt I feel when the prevailing element hits me, for I will never be the same, it changes my original form. I am no longer what I used to be. For the fire changes me, making me evolve into something bigger and better. A blacksmith, when he shapes iron or metal, uses various tools to bend, hammer, and cut it in its nonliquid form, then heats it until it glows, allowing forging to happen, this is what I must experience in order to grow.

Hot forging is done at a high temperature which makes metal easier to shape and less likely to fracture. Through this heat wave of a storm, God is attempting to shape me into what I am intended to be. Ultimately, making me less fragile with time and when life presents me with other misfortunes, and it will, I will be even more equipped to deal. He is providing me with metal armor of sorts, in order to keep my glow-finding ways to inspire the same in others.

I light a spark for having my best interest at heart, giving me a glint of hope that tomorrow will be a new day and I promise to leave a light for others to follow.

I am fire! Burn baby, burn.

Reflection Prompt: Your Own Journey Through the Elements

In "The Elements, Fire Prevails," the poet speaks of life's challenges as a forge — a powerful heat that reshapes and strengthens us. The elements— air, earth, water, and fire—mirror the forces that move through our own lives: breath and love, grounding and living, tears and healing, fire and transformation.

Now, take a moment to reflect on your own journey through the elements:

- What moments in your life have felt like fire — times of change, challenge, or growth?
- How has this "fire" shaped who you are today?
- What element do you feel closest to right now — air, earth, water, or fire — and why?
- How might you carry your "glow" forward, to light the way for others?

Write freely — there is no right or wrong way to respond. Let the elements speak through you.

Pride

Be black,

Gay,
Muslim,
Jew,
Overweight,
Poor,
Uneducated,
But grow up hearing that you need to take pride in your
Heritage,
Self,
Religious views,
Body image,
Circumstance,
Education,
With the hopes of having a inner emotion that is satisfies the choices one
makes, And overwhelming sense of belonging,
Being full of praise-
Even after you look in the mirror,
You love yourself and accept your own and
BE.
However society has a different mirror,
That looks back at you and
Judges,
Points fingers,
Laughs,
Dismisses,
And is bewildered that you were taught such a thing,
For only the
White,

Straight,
Christian,
Protestant,
Skinny,
Rich,
And Educated can have pride.
Feeling lied to,
The blacks become aggressive,
The gays march, fully colored to be seen,
The Muslims and the Jews fight over righteousness and become indignant,
The overweight turn into alpha males and mean girls,
The poor steal,
The uneducated drop out of school,
All in search of Pride!
Pride promised by
Their parents.
Just when you thought the emotional heartache of finding out there was
really no Santa Claus,
Easter Bunny,
Tooth fairy,
Was disappointing,

You are faced with a loss of Pride?
And left with
SHAME.
How do they restore and mend their promised pride?
Reverse the mirror and let them
BE!

Reflection Prompt

"Pride" challenges us to think about identity, belonging, and the mirrors society holds up to us. Reflect: What mirrors have shaped how you see yourself? Where have you found pride—and where has it been denied? How might you "reverse the mirror" for yourself or for others?

Fragile

Characterized as being fragile, easily broken.

She even captured how fragile I was by saying her interactions with me are like a bull being in a china cabinet.

So I poured on the superglue and fell back. Knowing full well that two hard people cause friction.

One cannot apologize for being soft when dealing with a woman; however, if that is a sign of weakness for her, the superglue has closed the wounds and allowed me to proceed in a safer, cautious, and functional manner.

Call me durable from now on.

Reflection Prompt

Fragility and strength can coexist in surprising ways. Reflect: When have you felt fragile yet resilient? How do you navigate vulnerability in your relationships? What does being "durable" mean to you after healing from past wounds?

A Change in My Story

I am honored to have been...
Exposed to abuse,
Able to see my mother beaten and lose her dignity,
A victim of childhood sexual abuse,
Adorned with the perils of alcoholism.
I am honored to have been...
Unconquerable, despite not growing with middle-class funds,
Thankful enough to have been exposed to middle-class values,
Grateful to a father who had the financial means and decorated career to
have lifted me from lower class financial status but chose to care for two
white children who were not his and only respected him for tangible gifts
he provided.

These experiences...
Helped me recognize signs of abuse, making me skillful in protecting my
children and the children of others,
Understand what it means to drink socially,
Seek relationships that compliment my authentic higher self,
Raise children who care more about exemplifying good character and
kindness, rather than material things,
Appreciative of fathers who extend themselves to ensure their children are
protected and provided for.
Hence,

I am honored to...
Release what no longer serves me,
Embrace my new colorful aura,
Celebrate God's power and spirit,
Take the Big Leap to find and live my personal legend,
Know Rei and Ki,
And live in an abundance of love, light, money and creativity,

All which grow in
Harmony.
The new story has a resounding ring.

Reflection Prompt

Our stories shape us, but they don't define us forever. Reflect: What parts of your past have helped you grow and protect what matters most? How have you released what no longer serves you? What new story are you choosing to live now?

Sterling Silver

My eyes fill with tears
Thinking of Alton Sterling--
Sterling, a name that means valuable for your efforts, your works, your qualities.
As he lay on the asphalt being shot execution style,
The Sterling tarnishes, not because he was exposed to air or moisture but because two people who were supposedly trained to protect and serve didn't see his value, his luster.
As a mother of three black young men,
I see their faces and look for the polish, the cloth that would keep them shiny so they do not encounter a moment where they are seen as a faux human, artificial, blackened Sterling.

Reflection Prompt

This poem honors the value and dignity of a life lost too soon. Reflect: How do you recognize and protect the worth in yourself and others—especially in the face of injustice? What actions can you take to help preserve the "shine" in those you care about?

Oasis

A fertile spot was found in the desert and it gave life, again. A rebirth, a new vision,
Letting the thoughts flow from within.
Power, strength, vitality,
Circulate as one drinks from the spring.
Giving all that is required,
Love,
Creativity,
Harmony,
And Offering.
Shine.
And seek refuge and growth in the greenery that surrounds.
The one who sends
Light
And
Love
Abound.
Is waiting for you to follow your heart,
As that is where the treasure is found.

Reflection Prompt

An oasis offers life and renewal in unexpected places. Reflect: Where do you find your own oasis—places or moments that restore your strength and creativity? How do you follow your heart to discover the treasures within?

A New Year

The beauty about anything new is that it is fresh, crisp, and open to possibilities.
I look forward to all that the New Year has to offer.
I can smell the cleanliness and purity and
taste the crisp fruit that were once seeds of thought.
I can hear the knock on the doors that open to the Oasis of freedom--
creating a sacred circle for healing to touch countless lives. My eyes are open to see what God has intended me and them to be.
I sense nothing but greatness.

Reflection Prompt

New beginnings hold the promise of growth and healing. Reflect: What fresh possibilities are you welcoming into your life? How do you stay open to the gifts a new chapter can bring? What hopes do you carry into your own "sacred circle" this year?

Live Longer, See Clearer

The older you are,
The wiser you become,
And you cannot relegate your elevated wisdom to your inflated intelligence
quotient but rather,
Your eyes tell of experiences, a visual witness.
Since you have this aged wisdom, you have an extreme desire to advise the
young.
To step in, say, "Stop, I've seen this before, I can even tell you exactly how
this story will end." Then, you remember they deserve the same
experiences, the same insight, the ability to earn their Wisdom Eyes--
finding peace, harmony, and enlightenment.

Reflection Prompt

This poem reflects on the wisdom that comes with age and experience,
emphasizing how true insight is seen through "wisdom eyes" rather than
just intelligence. Reflect on a moment when you wished you could warn
someone younger—or yourself—about a challenge or mistake. How do
you balance the desire to guide others with allowing them to learn through
their own journeys? What does "wisdom" mean to you beyond just
knowledge?

Female Porcupine

She's a human porcupine.
Her sharp quills and spines protect her from predators.
They have been there for years but with each year, each experience, each
hurt, they grow longer, thicker.
Sometimes they break off but as soon as she feels even a small hint of
vulnerability, new quills grow, making the distance even longer so no one
gets close to her.
That's what makes her even more fascinating, more curious, and the
observer's interest grows just as fast as her quills. One craves for her and
only the extreme patient, persistent mate will claim her as a booty, a most
valuable prize.
Maybe the quills aren't just there to protect her but to protect anyone of
interest?
Maybe the sharpness is a warning.?...
I am difficult to love.
I will break your heart.
I have been broken.
She leaves to find a habitat 2,691 miles, 39 hours away, and hides in the
mountains, just in case her sharp spines won't scare you away. She will hide
in the mountains so you cannot find her. She wants you to give up and you
do.
Although you capitulate, you are succumbed with a spirit of gratitude, and
are left with panoramic images of what could have been.
Every now and then, a thought will cross your mind and a smile will come
across your face but it will give you the spirit to endure life's obstacles
because the largest one, you couldn't conquer.
Nothing else can stand in your way.
For you are protected.

Reflection Prompt

This poem uses the metaphor of a porcupine to explore the ways we protect ourselves from pain and vulnerability. Reflect on how past experiences shape the emotional "quills" you or others carry. How do protective barriers both guard and isolate us? What might it take for someone to gently approach or heal those wounds? Have you ever had to decide whether to keep your distance or try to get close despite the risks?

The Winnings

I fell asleep the night before feeling as if I had already won,
As if it was owed to me,
Only to wake up feeling it was a charge from the Source,
Reminding me that I have a duty to help and heal people of the world,
Using health and wellness,
Providing spiritual guidance,
Shining light on darkness,
Modeling unconditional love,
Cultivating a culture of creativity,
and using the winnings to build our sacred space, The Oasis.
A space where the sick visit and leave healed, multiplying my winnings
through humanity---benevolent riches!

Reflection Prompt

This poem explores the evolving nature of friendships over time—the joy
of finding true companions, the pain of losing others, and the wisdom
gained through these experiences. Reflect on your own journey with
friendship. How have your friendships changed as you've grown? What
qualities do you now value most in friends? How do you handle the loss or
change of relationships as life moves forward?

Words Are Your Jam

Words are definitely your jam.
You string them together, making all who have the honor to read them sweet like jam. Soften like jam.
Freed from the restricted places where they once felt jammed.
Initiating musical, rhythmic, sounds, sparking a somatic movement and shouting, " This is my jam!" Jovially activating magical, "jam" sessions to hold and be held.
Journey.
Advocate,
Medicinally.
The plants, the ancestors, the people are resonating resoundingly to this jam.
Spirit's Elements
I ask God daily to heal the wounds so we can see, hear, touch, smell, and taste each other's goodness again. To see the person we think we are and how we show up to the world. To be able to hear and speak our truth regardless of the circumstances and in the right spirit. To seek to understand and then be understood. To touch each other with the softness that is in alignment of love. To smell the aromas of gratitude and whatever we are cooking in the pot these days, feel the warmth that provides. To taste whatever is being served, with love, compassion, and sensuality.
May water cleanse the wounds.
May air blow away the negativity from our minds.
May fire purify us spiritually, that we can see the Spirit and Goddess in each other.
May the abundance of that the earth provides, remind us of the abundance we can provide for and to each other.
May our ancestors be rooting for us.
Asé

Reflection Prompt

This poem speaks about the realization that true "winning" is not just personal success but a responsibility to serve and uplift others through healing, love, and creativity. Reflect on what "winning" means to you beyond material gains. How do you see your successes contributing to the greater good or helping others? What kind of "sacred space" do you want to create in your life or community.

tWitch

...to give or cause to give a short, sudden jerking or convulsive movement
Or perhaps purposefully redefined, to give a short, sudden, convulsive
message to spark a movement?
A movement that creates an atmosphere of vulnerability.
A movement which sheds light on confronting our shadows.
A movement that, while one can light up a room, darkness can be lurking
in the depths of one's soul. A movement which takes the stigma away.
A movement that brings awareness to the causes, subtle signs, and action
steps necessary to extend and provide comfort. A movement which takes
those who have risen to a level where all the onlookers are in awe. Not
knowing...his life will become..
A movement.
It is essential that we combine the "that" and the "which."
Instead of shouting wake up,
From now on, I choose to shout...
tWitch
to bring awareness to the movement
To jerk the souls of the people
Until their bodies convulse
and their foundation shakes
And twitches...
sparking a healing movement so the community can lead a life that was
intended for them.

Creative & Reflective Prompt

This poem explores the power of a sudden, sharp movement—both physical and metaphorical—as a catalyst for awareness, healing, and confronting hidden struggles. Reflect on a moment in your life when a sudden realization, event, or "twitch" sparked change or growth. How did that moment shake your foundation or awaken a new perspective? Consider the idea of vulnerability as a strength rather than a weakness. How can moments of discomfort or revelation inspire healing, both personally and within your community? Write about or discuss the movements—big or small—that have led you or others toward deeper awareness and transformation.

Focus on the We, Not the They

George a name that means "tiller of soil"
Floyd, a name that means "gray"
His brutal death is a reminder that
Black people in America need their own.
We need our own soil.
We need to plant our own seeds.
We need a place where we can accept our own and be ourselves.
We need to be farmers, to manage our own land so that we can till the soil
by breaking the cycle of racism because...
They think they are invincible,
They think they can take away the first gift God ever gave us, breath,
They would rather see us die than have liberty,
They will continue to see "gray" smoke in their cities across the country
until they feel the same pain, heartache, and suffering that WE experience
daily.
They like to take the second meaning of the color gray, without interest or
character.
They show their mental and moral qualities and are given grace time after
time.
We have to fight back 'till' we can only see black, as the "gray" is too
passive and the white cannot get it right.
I write this in remembrance of our brother, George Floyd.

Reflective & Analytical Prompt

This poem calls for unity, self-determination, and resilience within the Black community, emphasizing the importance of cultivating one's own "soil" and breaking cycles of oppression. Reflect on the meaning of "focus on the we, not the they" in your own life or community. How does centering collective strength and ownership empower people facing systemic challenges? Consider the impact of historical and ongoing injustices referenced in the poem, such as the deaths of George Floyd and others, and how they inspire movements for change. Write or discuss ways communities can nurture their own growth, healing, and liberation despite external resistance.

Burdens Are Not Meant for You to Bear

Born , and knowingly created to endure a governing body upon his
shoulders.
A son, embodied with the same power as the largest, nearest star in the
universe,
The sun.
Emitting a light and a stillness of sovereignty,
Inspiring Admiration,
Guidance, eternal serenity,
That only a father could provide.
In order to rule as the chief leader of the land,
spreading justice, amid the injustice.
Cultivating righteousness, in pursuit of the wicked who crookedly are
unable to define what is straight,
Losing their way, their direction,
succumbed by the divine ordained, spiritual pestilence in the land.
A call to action that would make anyone run from their purpose, duty and
targeted assignment.
For it is too much to bear in pursuit of peace.
And so the external and internal struggles ensue.
Experiences of privilege, blind to injustices
Observing the tennis match between the races of people who string cords
and cause a racket; With each hit, the souls become hollow centered.
The governing body continues to get the upper hand, the momentum,
causing the righteous to surrender to struggle.
Unable to witness the game meant to destroy generations of original
people who are now gift-blinded, deaf to the racially-charged ruckus,
Have muted voices, reduced intellect
The effects.
The purpose-driven Prince had seen enough.
Prophetic passionate phrases poured onto the people,

Opened their ears
to hear, their eyes to see, and their mouths to sing the pleasant praises of
the Prince who is a
Wonderful
Mighty
Everlasting
Counselor
God
Father and
promoter of Peace.
The burdens of the people lifted.

Reflection Prompt: The Calling to Lead and the Weight of Burdens

This poem evokes the image of a leader called to shine like the sun—
radiating light, justice, and peace—yet grappling with the weight of
responsibility and generational struggle. It reminds us that some burdens
are too great to bear alone and that divine strength and communal
awakening are needed.

 Reflect on a time when you or someone you admire was called to take on
a role or responsibility that felt overwhelming. How did they (or you)
confront this burden? What spiritual, communal, or internal resources
provided strength? Write about the tension between duty and self-
preservation—and the moments when burdens are finally lifted.

The Medicine

I know it's sacred when even in my darkest of hours,
I say repeatedly to the Spirit, " Thank you for everything."
I know it's sacred when I am losing everything and I still feel at peace.
I know it's sacred when I find myself in spaces and places I never thought
were in reach.
I know it's sacred when being among the plants proves to be more
comforting than people.
I know it's sacred when I place it in my hand and feel the pull to ask for
permission to use.
I know it's sacred when my people find me and I am no longer chasing but
becoming Spirit's magnet.
I know it's sacred when I look forward to the elements that help me find
my way back to the roots of the Earth, the flow of the water, the fire's
phases of transformation, and inhaling/exhaling air regulates my body to
feel true freedom and liberation.
I know it's sacred when the middle (medi) of the cine (movie) is my life
with pictures in motion.
I know it's sacred when my brain turns to mush to make room for the
blessings without end.
I know it's sacred.
I know it's medicine.
I know it's Spirit.
I know it's liberating.
I know it's freedom.
I know it's healing the collective to be in service to others so our mother's
mothers and our father's fathers lineage forms a line of family that ages
with the wisdom found in our indigenous traditional spiritual practices.
For I know the plans, the prosperity and the hope for the future.
I know, I know, I know...
in the liberating depths of my soul.

Prompt: Discovering Sacred Medicine

Write about a time when you found comfort, healing, or peace in something unexpected—whether it be nature, spirit, rituals, or a feeling of deep gratitude during hardship. Explore how this "medicine" brought you closer to a sense of freedom, liberation, or connection. What makes this medicine sacred to you? How does it guide you back to your roots, your true self, or a higher power? Reflect on the transformative power of embracing this healing force in your life.

Zion

In a thankless school leadership position, I am always looking to find the light, amid the darkness.
The highest point in my day is when I see the face of Zion,
A face whose skin is like darken tree bark
After being doused in rain after the night's storm,
It is as if the twenty-five other fires I had to respond or attend to are immediately extinguished,
Like when you are learning the alphabet and you finally get it to and master the twenty-sixth letter
Z,
You are positively charged with an ion of energy that makes you sing
In your Lauryn Hill voice.
Z–ion.
Now, the joy of my day is in Zion.
Reminding me that what I do is bigger than me.
What I do is fueled by the faces of young people who light up because
I simply showed up.
It is the unspoken, unconditional admiration and innocence
That is backed by a steep, massive mountain that allows me to focus on
spiritually elevating others to keep climbing toward the summit,
Though it may be rocky,
I may be graced and blessed with a face of Zion.
And if am granted such an opportunity,
I know I am on the right path,
One of favor.
Instead of looking for the hills,
I will bend my neck a little further to the mountains,
A holy place.
The Kingdom of Zion.

Prompt: Finding Light in Leadership

Write about a challenging role or responsibility where you often feel overwhelmed or underappreciated. Describe the moments or people—like the face of Zion in the poem—that remind you why you keep going and give you renewed energy and purpose. How do these sparks of light help you rise above the difficulties and stay focused on a higher calling or mission? Reflect on the ways you find spiritual or emotional elevation amid the struggles.

Colored Purple

The black and blue bruises that link us to the path of healing are told in our stories.
Stories told are vibrations of oration that heal the unhealed parts of ourselves.
There in the stores is the medicine, the antidote of the poisonous events women have endured and continue to live in the shades of shame.
For some of us, we continue to be voiceless.
For others, we rock or sacral pelvises to garner the attention of men in an effort that they might provide a reciprocal comfort and nourishment which was abandoned during our developmental years.
And then there are those who carry their pain in their expanded bodies, a weight of protection. The bold bodies come with boisterous outspoken colored utterances.
Utterances that our masculine counterparts do not allow and we are beaten to submission to remain a phonically silent to remind us of our place,
The bedroom, the kitchen, or tend to the children.

Through the stories we find strength that penetrates our internal souls.
Going inward with perfect and purposeful introspection.
We go carrying the deceptive red blood flowing to our hearts, the blood our ancestors shed, the blood that appears indigo in our veins
And with every heartbeat…
Lub dub (F)
Lub dub (O)
Lub dub (R)
Lub dub (G)
Lub dub (I)
Lub dub (V)
Lub dub (E)
…we eventually learn true love requires us to forgive.

So we can see our culturally black bruises of red and blue show us the
Magic, peace, and pride
in The Color Purple.

Next time you see it, take a deep breath in,
Open your mouth and let it go,
the voiced story
becomes the medicine for our sisters.

Prompt: Healing Through Our Stories
Write about the power of sharing personal or collective stories as a path to
healing—especially stories that reveal pain, resilience, and strength. Reflect
on how voicing your truth or listening to the truths of others can
transform shame into pride, silence into empowerment, and wounds into
medicine. How does forgiveness play a role in this journey? Consider the
symbolism of "color" in your healing process and what it represents for
you or your community.

Releasing the Timid Spirit

Wondrous working power lives in our God-given spirit so why are you afraid to express yourself authentically with a forward bravery to influence the people of the world in a loving kindness spirit of discipline?
When you do you
Honor God.
So walk in the room, no matter the audience, with confidence, esteem and with every step movement, words spoken, whisper to your soul giving God the thanks that he embodied you with attributes that are reflective of him. When the accolades come, this time shout to the rooftops, mountains and skies thanking the father and listen to the call and response he returns, "Well done my good and faithful servant."
Calling you to do more of his work and he will bless you with words of affirmation and validation for following doing his will.
Focus on what he planted in you,
Believe that believe is an action verb,
Make your acts powerful, loving and controlled.
Creating a new PLC-powerful, loving, community.

Prompt: Embracing Your God-Given Power with Courage

Within each of us lives a spirit filled with divine strength and purpose, yet fear often holds us back from fully expressing our authentic selves. Reflect on what it means to release timidity and step boldly into your God-given gifts—walking confidently, speaking truthfully, and living with loving discipline.

How does embracing this courage honor your faith and inspire those around you? Write about the journey from fear to fearless faith, and how trusting in God's affirmation empowers you to build a powerful, loving community.

Section 2

The Dance of Connection: Navigating Love, Friendship, and Relationships

This section explores the various dynamics of relationships, from romantic love to family bonds and friendships. The poems here delve into the balance between giving and receiving, the pain of distance or neglect, and the profound impact others have on our lives.

Loving with Gratitude

Love,
You have to respect it or it will come back and bite you like a hunted animal under attack.
Respect the one you love and respect the love of others.
Sometimes you encounter people who possess characteristics that you may fall in love with; however, only one person seeks all of the benefits.
You smile, because you want for others, what you want for yourself.
The irony is that sometimes when someone else is going through troubles, they inspire you. The worst time in their lives, becomes the best time in yours.
You are ultimately grateful.

Reflection Prompt

Love asks for respect — of self, of others, and of the journey each person is on. Reflect: How have your experiences with love taught you about respect? Have you ever been inspired by another's struggle? How do gratitude and empathy shape the way you love today?

Distance

I understand the distance but
It magnifies the surreal connection.
I understand the complications but
The peace and clarity you provide align my thoughts.
I understand the withdrawal but
To stay provides fervor to the heated heartiness which feeds my
abundant appetite. I understand the emotional struggle but
Giving in allows me to breathe again.
Wait, perhaps I don't understand?
This isn't about me but rather, your trajectory.
So be distant if you need to fasten or secure your inner connection,
Work through your complexities in order to gain insight,
Be withdrawn so you can find your way and feed your soul,
Accept your emotional struggle, so that you shake your very foundation
releasing a spirit of favored freedom. Now, I understand.
Twenty-One
Brass, the gift one gets after 21 years of marriage. Bring out the brass
instruments.
The trombones,
The trumpets,
The tubas,
A celebration is in order.
An order ordained by God.

Reflection Prompt

Distance can challenge or deepen connection. Reflect: When have you needed distance — or given it to someone else — in order to grow? How has time apart shaped your understanding of love, connection, or freedom? What does it mean to celebrate connection after space has been honored?

YOU

You inspire me!
You cure my low moments.
You make me see the goodness in others.
You challenge my thinking.
You tell me what I do not wish to hear.
You compliment me, figuratively and literally. You nurse my hurts.
You allow me to express my thoughts.
You give me permission to breathe easier.
You protect me from harm.
You grant me the permission to be me.
If only we could use a conjunction to link the pronouns You and I.

Reflection Prompt

Think about the "You" in your life — the person or people who inspire you, challenge you, and allow you to be fully yourself. Who comes to mind? How have they shaped your growth and understanding of connection? What might it look like to truly link "You" and "I"?

She is

She is..
Emotionally giving,
Giving me everything I desire,
Desiring more and more each passing day,
As the days increase, the expectation as well and she always rises to the occasion, Occasions, each of them, give reason, purpose, making me want to hold those moments in time. Time will shape and cultivate a relationship that will withstand and surpass rationale, seasons, and lifetimes. A lifetime, the duration that I pray she will be with me (us), Me is she and she is me.
Together, we are one.

Reflection Prompt

We often long for authenticity in others — and in ourselves. Reflect: How do you respond when people show only a surface version of themselves? How do you balance your desire for authenticity with acceptance? What does it mean to you to "accept people for who they are and what they are willing to give"?

Grandfather

Always providing a comic relief,
A contagious, nurturing energy,
That makes you feel like you have no worries in the world. And if you
do,
They should not be of concern.
Occasionally, amid the jokes and storytelling,
He drops seeds of wisdom,
The decadence of worldly issues,
From the economy, race relations, social constructs, and politics. But, he
doesn't stay there.
He transitions from the serious tone,
Moving from that avenue to a boulevard of bliss, Prompting us to
recollect what is important in life,
 Balancing beatitudes,
We may weep now but we shall and will laugh again. Grateful for you,
Granddaddy!

Reflection Prompt

Grandparents often hold wisdom wrapped in laughter and stories.
Reflect: Who in your life has been a source of comfort, joy, and guidance
like this grandfather? What lessons have they shared that you carry with
you? How do you balance the serious and joyful moments in your
relationships?

The Rib Cage

In awe,
Then move to hysterically laughing
When people tell me they are so in love but consequently,
They are regulated to rules.
Rules that affect choices.
The choosing of friends,
Who can call or text,
And even with the approved list,
The other party has permission to go through their electronic devices,
Taking cloud surveillance to a whole other level.
A relationship where you can be called out of your name or told who can
come visit the home you both share. Or who can be in your company?
All is overlooked because your financial portfolio is more important than
your personal freedom. So you compromise your integrity, barter
internally with God, and pray it gets better. Or that they get some
confidence that makes them more secure.
A doctor may tell the silent abuser that the rib cage already protects the
heart,
No need to put her in a cage for it limits her and all she can be to you.
Why the cage?
What are you afraid of?
Perhaps she isn't yours anyway?
The rib cage even gives permission for the heart to expand.

Reflection Prompt

This poem explores how two lovers—one of words, one of love—come together to inspire creativity and growth. Reflect: How have your relationships (romantic or otherwise) influenced your personal or creative journey? In what ways can opening yourself to connection help you discover new parts of yourself and your passions? What does "dancing" freely with others mean to you?

This poem uses the metaphor of a rib cage to explore control, freedom, and love within relationships. Reflect on the balance between love and personal freedom: Have you ever experienced or witnessed boundaries in a relationship that felt like a cage rather than protection? What fears or insecurities might cause someone to control a partner? How can love allow space to grow instead of limiting it?

Worst Friend

Treated like an object or even a favorite book,
You pick me up when you wanna play,
Or read me again to reminisce,
But I'm human.
I have emotions, feelings, and needs.
Am I to put those aside until the impulse hits you to notice me again.
Hoping you will dry my tears, listen to how I am feeling, and respond to
my needs, not just when it's convenient for you. You are the worst
friend!

Reflection Prompt

This poem explores the pain of feeling used and undervalued in a
friendship, treated more like an object than a person with feelings.
Reflect on a time when you felt neglected or taken for granted by
someone close to you. How did that experience affect your view of
friendship and your boundaries? What do you believe true friendship
should look and feel like?

Catharsis

When I converse with him, the endorphins that are released in my mind are immeasurable. As if every pain or hurt I have ever experienced, despite being buried in the depths of my soul, vanishes. I am grateful and appreciative to have known and been blessed with such a presence....my cathartic comfort.

Silence, So Loud

He said he would call, but I never heard from him.

The silence is intentional, purposeful.

Who would use this tactic in order to omit mention, pretend I don't exist?Ignore me, hoping I will go away. Today, your wish came true.

Bye

Mirroring silence, too!

Out of the blue, I hear from you.

One word, one liners, that somehow draws me back in knowing I'm not the one for you.

Reflection Prompt

This poem captures the deep emotional release and healing found in connection with someone special, but also the pain when that connection turns to silence and absence. Reflect on a relationship in your life that brought you both comfort and challenge. How did that relationship impact your emotional well-being? How do you cope when someone important withdraws or disappears?

Fear of Rejection

I'm not sure when I learned this pattern
But at some point in my life I must have been rejected.
It must have hurt so bad that I buried it in the depths of my soul.
However, it follows me and prevents me from maintaining meaningful
relationships.
I am hypersensitive—so much so that when someone does the slightest
thing,
I believe it was done intentionally to hurt or destroy me.
Crazy, huh?
I know.
So I begin to take steps back,
As they move closer,
I step back,
Until they are so far away from me,
I become a distant blurred memory of their past.
I'm not sure what they are thinking,
They are blindsided and are left in a cloud of bewilderment.
All because I could not find the courage to be vulnerable enough to
share that my feelings were hurt. Or to even give the other party the
benefit of the doubt by questioning them about said event?
I will never know.
They will never know.
We both just fade to black.
The hurt on the surface disappears or is marked unknown.
The soul is tattooed with bruises the next victim never sees until fear and
rejection reappear.
Spurning.

Reflective & Personal Growth Prompt

This poem explores how early experiences of rejection can create deep emotional patterns that affect our ability to connect with others. Reflect on a time when fear of rejection or vulnerability has influenced your relationships or interactions. How does this fear shape the way you respond to others' actions—real or perceived? Consider what it might take to break this cycle of withdrawing and misinterpretation. Write about ways to build courage for vulnerability and honest communication, or discuss how healing from past hurts can open space for deeper connections.

A True Friend

At some times in your life, you are surrounded by a multitude of beings
you call friends.
As you grow and develop and become more steadfast in your prayer on
and to the wise,
Those who you thought that had a sparkling smile when they saw you,
You came to learn, they were none the wiser about the true meaning of
friendship.

When that reality hits,
You fall to your knees, close your eyes and surrender to the trials and it
is then and only then you understand who and whose friendship you can
most rely on.

Such divinely called submission brings an authentic smile to your face, an
unconditional love envelopes your heart space, and you take long walks
to talk with your friend.

He listens and the words are safe under lock and key, where the locked
box is only opened by him when your foundation has been shaken to
remind you of who you are and whose you are.

His friend.

Your discernment is now more selective and you now see people who
share that same friend.
We collectively share unspoken heards.
An endearing quality we learned from our sacredly shared friend.
That's when you know you know,
True friendship.

Spiritual Reflection & Personal Growth Prompt

This poem reflects on the evolving understanding of friendship through life's trials and spiritual deepening. It highlights how adversity and prayer can clarify which friendships are genuine and enduring, ultimately pointing to a divine friendship that offers unwavering comfort and guidance. Reflect on a time when life experiences reshaped your understanding of friendship. Who has proven to be a true friend in your life—human or divine? How do trust, discernment, and shared spiritual values influence the relationships you choose to nurture? Write about what it means to you to be, and to have, a true friend.

Training Our Children

Even at the moment of conception, move in love.
As the baby is developing in the womb, read with expression.
For every month that passes, be intentional in your ways, rituals and routines.
Along the way, ask God for symbols and signs of what the name should be.
A first and the middle.
The first will speak to the character, the middle will be how they show up in the world.
For a name that has meaning, a child will want to live up to upon the arrival.
Once born, the first five years are vitally important.
Teach and talk to the child with compassion.
Refer to the child in reverence.
Adorn the child with blessed clothes.
Inspire the child with intellectual resources, tools, structures and systems.
Nourish and nurture the child to feed on the finest foods and the favored word.
This way, when you send them off in the worldly, world,
When they fall or fail, they will find comfort in the teachings,
Pithy pieces of advice
Located in the core of their souls.
For which they will rely upon forever and ever.

Prompt: Nurturing with Intention and Love

Raising children is a sacred journey that begins long before birth, filled with intentional acts, love, and hope. Reflect on the ways we prepare and guide the youngest generation—not just through words and actions, but through the values and wisdom we pass down.

How can names, rituals, and early teachings shape a child's character and future? What kinds of love, respect, and nourishment do you believe are essential in the first years of life?

Write about the power of intentional parenting or caregiving and the lasting impact it has on a child's soul and their ability to navigate the world.

God's Goddess

Two different stories told.
One enduring, a show of admiration,
making the listener enamored with the thoughts of enamoring another, a
comfort.

The public story told was quite different.
The listener, who was an intricate character in the story, was reduced to a
black magic root doctor.

At first hearing, anger ensued.
Then, in her mind's eye, she visualized his body retracting from the 180
degree lying down position, to the 90 degree angle,
as she rides,
he convulses,
ejaculating repeatedly as to lead him to a path of truth.
So orgasmic!
So witness worthy!
So, lie slayer-live the truth in silence and let your internal demons prevail.

The character who was reduced,
is in the blossom of God,
being comforted,
in the most authentic way--
admired, endeared, enamored,
Always.

Prompt: Exploring Dual Narratives and Authentic Power

Write about the experience of living between two contrasting stories—one told publicly, misunderstood or misrepresented, and the other deeply personal and empowering. How do you reconcile the external judgments with your own truth and inner strength? Explore the transformative power of embracing your authentic self, even when it challenges societal perceptions, and the quiet victory of living your truth in silence and confidence.

Section 3

Seeking and Releasing: A Quest for Peace, Truth, and Freedom

This section focuses on the inward journey of seeking and releasing—letting go of pain, finding truth, and pursuing spiritual or personal freedom. The poems here use metaphors of healing, searching, and new beginnings to illustrate this process.

A Revelation

I immediately popped up from my usual Sunday relaxation time. And just as clear as a picture on the most high-end HD television set, I saw it and took a deep breath.

Flashes of my relationships flash before me, brief frames. Almost as if I had a clicker in my hand with my thumb pushing the forward button rapidly, continuously.

Each frame had an undercurrent, a common theme which was that I have an extreme desire to get to know everyone's true, authentic self. Much like a drug addict fiends for her next score, that is my goal. However, it comes with a fatal flaw.

When people come into my life and continue to give me what they want society to see, the personality that is driven by ego, they no longer exist in my mind and are thrown away like garbage.

Do I interact with them? Yes, on the surface. Do I give them opportunities to make mistakes? Sure, I do. I want that same consideration.

The irony is that those who come into my life and give me glimpses of who they really are, they are able to make a multitude of mistakes and they still remain in my circle of love.

The fake, the fraudulent, the counterfeit, and the dummy don't get the same consolation because to me they are inhuman. I am left with the question,"Am I the inhuman one?" Or am I searching for glimpses of God-Like qualities in others? Today, I will put away my experiential thinking and just accept people for who they are and what they are willing to give.

Reflection Prompt

Love can be deeper and more lasting than others may realize.
Reflect: Have you ever loved, admired, or respected someone in a
way that endured beyond time or distance? How do you honor your
own capacity for love, even when it is misunderstood? What does
"staying power" mean to you?

Only When I am Ready To Read

The pain has morphed into a favorite backpack where one feels comforted and familiar with it.

So much so that along the way they add to the backpack as if they are building a library of books where they learn about the same pain over and over again.

The backpack gets heavier and physiologically their joints begin to hurt, hips get wider, and they stack on the pounds to hide. Someone sends them light and love,

They gain mental clarity,

But when it's time to remove the collection of resources and venture off into a new section of the library,

They freeze and panic because the books filled with pain have been well read and comfortable,

They do not feel equipped to read any other book, almost like an emergent reader who thinks that the words in the two or three books they read don't appear in other books.

The healer lets the pain stay there, until the client is ready to let go of it and is open to new books, with new high frequency words which will make the pain go away.

But only when they are ready to read.

Reflection Prompt

Pain can become a familiar companion, even when it weighs us down. Reflect: When have you felt comforted by old pain, even as it held you back? What does "being ready" to let go mean to you? How might you support yourself or others in opening to new chapters of healing?

Crash

Escaping
Rushing, busy
Instead of taking a moment to stop and smell the roses
The sounds, alerts, and ringtones from my cell phone give me
another reason to go. Going became symbolic of letting go
Letting go of stresses
Letting go of rejection
Letting go of insecurities
And one night when I let go a little having too much to drink
Made it home safely with a battered and bruised car
All because I fell asleep at the wheel, blacked out
My response today,
is to pause, slow down, stop to put the petals back together so I can
smell the roses again.

Reflection Prompt

In our fast-paced lives, we often forget to pause and appreciate the
small moments. Reflect: When have you felt the need to slow down
and "smell the roses"? How do you create space for rest and healing
after life's crashes? What steps can you take to reconnect with
yourself?

Prayer, Where are you?

Prayer changes things.
Will prayer change the lives of those who attended the prayer
meeting? Will prayer change how the world sees black lives?
Will prayer change our judgment of others who aren't like us?
Will prayer change the minds of the racist, the bigot, the
homophobic, and the sexist? Will prayer uplift people who are blind,
deaf and dumb?
Will prayer change how the black male is portrayed in the media?
Will prayer change the hypocrites who wear a badge that gives them
permission to kill?
If change is the most constant thing in the universe, I am depending
on you, Prayer.

Reflection Prompt

This poem asks us to consider the impact of prayer in a world filled
with injustice and pain. Reflect: What role does prayer—or your
own form of hope and intention—play in your life and in seeking
change? How do you hold onto faith when confronted with difficult
realities? In what ways can belief inspire action toward justice and
healing?

The Cycle of Friendship

As a youngster, I was quiet and selective when it came to making friends.

By middle school, the shyness disappears as quickly as a fake friend's love for you.

My personality, magnetic, although still very selective, I chose friends who thought they were better than me and maybe I believed them? And shunned those who would give up everything just to be in my presence.

Time, experience, and change provided a pathway of evolution that rounded my true friendships, creating a small, faithful circle. One would think that the travel of time would keep the friends in the circle but individually they are evolving, changing and relationships suffer losses. Grateful to the ones that can endure, sustain and have staying power. Good riddance to those who lost interest as I wish them well. And thank them for showing me who they are, releasing them to become who they are intended to be.

The cyclical camaraderie limits those who only want to surround themselves with people who are conformists, who think they are better, who shun. I used to be one of those but now I know better. I am selective, magnetic and surround myself with pieces of me.

Reflection Prompt

This poem captures the deep emotional release and healing found in connection with someone special, but also the pain when that connection turns to silence and absence. Reflect on a relationship in your life that brought you both comfort and challenge. How did that relationship impact your emotional well-being? How do you cope when someone important withdraws or disappears?

Our Prayer

I ask God daily to heal the wounds so we can see, hear, touch, smell, and taste each other's goodness again. To see the person we think we are and how we show up to the world. To be able to hear and speak our truth regardless of the circumstances and in the right spirit. To seek to understand and then be understood. To touch each other with the softness that is in alignment of love. To smell the aromas of gratitude and whatever we are cooking in the pot these days, feel the warmth that provides. To taste whatever is being served, with love, compassion, and sensuality.

May water cleanse the wounds.

May air blow away the negativity from our minds.

May fire purify us spiritually, that we can see the Spirit and Goddess in each other.

May the abundance of that the earth provides, remind us of the abundance we can provide for and to each other.

May our ancestors support us.

Asé

Reflective Prompt

This poem invites us to envision a world healed through connection, understanding, and sensory awareness. Reflect on the ways you experience and express love, truth, and compassion through your senses—sight, hearing, touch, smell, and taste. How might these senses deepen your relationships and your understanding of others? Consider the symbolic elements of water, air, fire, and earth as forces for healing and renewal in your life. What prayers or intentions would you offer for yourself, your community, or the world to cultivate more kindness and spiritual clarity?

The Leprechaun: God & Time

Have you ever seen a Jamaican Leprechaun?
He lurks behind the manicured bushes and flowering shrubs.
Unlike the traditional diminutive man,
He is thin and of average height.
This bearded man who rocks the color green to attract you to the
green weeds of grass native to his country, a sacred herb which
heightens your perception and senses, leading you to a euphoric
state.
With the hopes of collecting in return some of your green money to
build a life and during that life he will witness the glory of God in
Time.
Not a trickster, but a magician who innately knows the color green
reflects a worthiness of love, self, passion, and unconditional love.
He will **leap**.
Preach.
And **con**.Leprechaun..his way to get the bag, the treasure.
If you receive a call from him, know that it is not from God but a
reminder that God is not within our time, but he is within his own
time.
Wait I say, on Him.

Interpretive & Symbolic Prompt

This poem reimagines the figure of a leprechaun, blending cultural imagery, symbolism, and spiritual reflection. It explores themes of perception, value, deception, and the nature of divine timing. Reflect on the metaphor of the "Jamaican Leprechaun" and how it represents human desires, material pursuits, and spiritual awareness. What does it say about how we seek meaning, trust others, and wait for the right timing in life? Write about your own relationship with time, trust, and the pursuit of "treasures"—whether material or spiritual. How do you discern what is worth chasing, and when do you choose to wait?

Rest

Shifting focus to create and make space for the introspective
rumblings and calls to God where you believe have gone
unanswered.
Intentionally taking time to be still is when the answers come.
The work remains.
Take the time you need to re-set
And rest.
Or the evangelical wisdom you seek will be hidden behind the veil
of control that is navigating your life through lenses of hurt and
pain.
Relax and be still so the the inner workings of the mind, body, soul ,
and spirit can be
Restored!

Mindfulness & Spiritual Restoration Prompt

This poem emphasizes the transformative power of intentional
stillness and rest. It suggests that only by pausing and creating space
can we hear divine guidance and begin to heal from control, hurt,
and pain. Reflect on your own relationship with rest: When do you
give yourself permission to pause? What inner wisdom or answers
might be waiting for you in stillness? Write about a time when
stepping back and resting brought clarity, healing, or restoration to
your life. How can you more intentionally cultivate this practice
moving forward?

Peace in Overflow

The giving and receiving,
The herbal remedies of peace that come in the form of chamomile,
lavender, and the bay leaf that I lay on my heart so it's no longer
troubled.
Herbs of victory and peace.
In search of peace?
Just take a nature walk or find a trail of
The greenery,
Seek out thy gardens,
And the abundance of the land.
There you will find the symbols of peace left behind.
Go and leave fear, fearing your gifts that you will share with the
world.
With a few sips of cacao, cinnamon, and crushed cardamom, your
heart will no longer be troubled but open to receiving.
Peace overflows.

Nature's Remedies & Overflowing Peace Prompt

This poem reminds us that peace can be found in the natural world
and through simple rituals of care—herbs, teas, and the act of
walking in nature. It speaks to the healing that comes when we open
ourselves to receive. Reflect on the practices, places, or rituals that
bring you peace. How does nature restore you? What sensory
experiences—scents, tastes, textures—help soothe your spirit and
open your heart? Write about your personal recipe for finding
"peace in overflow" in your daily life.

Know the Plans

Each new year whether through a vision board, a pen and paper, or from the words we speak, we make plans for our future.
We identify what the year will hold.
Listing all things hoped for with tones of prosperity.
Success rooted in finances, professional advancements, and thriving in a substantial way.
This year, let's begin with a blank canvas.
One where we collect the blessings as they happen. The path will be made clear and you will be given direction from the most high, Divine guidance.
The discernment that protects you from harmful people, places, events.
In the end, you will see that hope turns to faith and your spiritually planned future is more than you imagined.
You see it!
Just let and allow him to direct and position you on your prosperous path.
After all, he mapped it out before your conception.
Now that you are here, let him do the same.

Prompt: Letting Go of Control—Trusting Divine Guidance

This poem invites a shift from rigid goal-setting to a posture of openness and trust—allowing life's blessings and direction to unfold through divine guidance rather than human planning.

Reflect on a time when you released control over a plan or expectation and allowed yourself to be guided by faith, intuition, or a higher power. What was that experience like? How did the outcome compare to what you originally envisioned?

Write about what it might feel like to approach a new year—or a new chapter of life—with an open canvas, collecting blessings and following the path as it is revealed.

Pleasing Faith

Sure, your celebrated milestones are major.
But it is your faith that you should be most proud of on this journey.
For the audience only sees the notable achievements,
not
the pain, repeated rejections, the misunderstandings, the shuns, the
gossip, the negative self-talk that you have heard in your brain, fed
by the trauma you endured that keeps reminding you of your
insecurities, uncertainties, depression, humiliation, unworthiness,
that you once believed was truth.
The significant allegiance is and loyalty belongs to the faith you had
to muster
It was only one to two millimeters in diameter.
A seed of bright yellow,
Where the spotlight shines on your trust and devotion to God.
Pleasing Faith.

Prompt: The Invisible Victory—Faith Through Struggle

This poem reminds us that the greatest triumphs are not always
visible to others—they live within the perseverance of our faith
through rejection, self-doubt, and hardship.
Reflect on a time when you had to hold on to faith—however
small—in the face of pain, rejection, or inner struggle. What
sustained you? How did your faith evolve through that experience?
How would you honor that invisible victory today?
Write about what pleasing faith means to you, and how it has shaped
your journey.

Renewed Strength

For every step taken, I grew weary.
For every marathon I have attempted to run, I was exhausted, ready to drop, empty.
I looked for new shoes, the Nike, the Hoka, in order to find a New Balance, any external gratification that I thought would make my walks energetically fresh.
Or a new outfit from LuLuLemon I could squeeze into which would make me run as fast as a train on speed.
Looking for a force outside of myself that I would somehow rise with action.

Out of nowhere I could hear my praying grandmother's voice saying, **"The force comes from within you, the force that created all living things is the force you are in search of. See the images of strength. Notice the evidence of hope. Consider who gave the eagle its size, power, strength, power-anointing to maneuver with agility and freedom."**

Therein lies the power of the ancestors and the connection with the Source, when their descendants have lost their way, their direction..
For when I lost hope, I heard God calling my name, instead of the converse.

And instantly I felt restored, renewed, resurrected to run grounded in the earth's power.

For every step taken, I feel refreshed.
For every test of endurance, strengthened.

For it is on his wings I fly and challenges abate.

Prompt: The True Source of Strength

We often look outward—toward new tools, new appearances, or external validation—when searching for strength or renewal. But as this poem reminds us, true power comes from within, rooted in faith, ancestral wisdom, and divine connection.

Reflect on a time when you were exhausted or discouraged and searched for external fixes. How did you eventually reconnect with your inner source of strength? What voices or wisdom—whether from ancestors, Spirit, or within—guided you?

Write about what it feels like to be "restored, renewed, resurrected" in your own life, and how you might trust this inner power more deeply going forward.

Bravery, Courage Within You

Awaken by the overthinking roller coaster of worries that shock
your brain into a mode of temporary paralysis.
You are terrified.
The precipitous life filled with razor-edged curves and
hypersensitive, emotional sudden changes that shock you into
submission.
You have tried to control everything.
I had to take you there. The place where you could hear your
heartbeat, and the effects that has on the air you breathe. Where
tears began to flow from your eyes like the rivers I created,
reminders of the ebb and flow of a purpose-driven journey.
When the roller coaster stops,
And your feet are no longer dangling high and moving back and
forth as if they were the mechanical controls operating the ride.
Your feet are safe on solid ground.
Flashes of the images you just experienced become still frames,
A stillness that nudges and speaks in a voice saying,
"I am with you wherever you go and that is what makes you
Strong
and
Brave."
Rescued to deliverance.

Prompt: Discovering Courage After the Storm

Sometimes life feels like an uncontrollable roller coaster—one that triggers fear, paralysis, and overwhelm. Yet it is often through these turbulent rides that we find our deepest strength and courage.
Reflect on a moment when fear or anxiety seemed to take over your life. What did that "ride" feel like emotionally and physically? How did you eventually find solid ground again? Who or what reminded you of the courage and bravery within you?
Write about the shift from fear to faith, and how the experiences that once terrified you may have ultimately prepared you for greater resilience and purpose.

A Divine Invitation

Spiritual paralysis sets in because when you
continue to receive the repeated majestic envelopes
That comes in the form of universal signs and symbols, that you
ignore since they come so frequently.
Taking the messages for granted, assuming they will always be there
when you are ready.
The thing is we are not promised tomorrow.
We have a deadline where we have to RSVP.
Call and response
A cue to stop
Whatever you are doing in that time, in that space and wake up and
pay attention
To the Divine Invitation.
and be initiated in the rituals and scriptures summoning you to
humble yourself and pray
Your wicked ways will turn, change directions
Open like the heavens' ear
The more that answer the call
The more forgiveness is granted
And the land will be healed.
Requiring awareness, action, and movement, an equation that leads
to healing.

Prompt: Responding to the Call of the Divine

We often receive subtle signs and messages from the universe—divine invitations calling us to awaken, reflect, and transform. Yet, how often do we ignore or postpone answering these sacred calls? Reflect on the urgency and importance of saying "yes" to the spiritual summons in your life.

What might it mean to humbly receive this invitation, change your ways, and actively participate in healing—both personally and collectively? Write about the power of awareness, response, and movement as keys to embracing your divine purpose and contributing to the healing of the world.

Thirst Calling

The gravitational pull to a modest and virtuous life,
In search for the free, perform or metabolic water source.
Distracted and side tracked by
The acorns that provide you with energy in the season of winter.
Or the cover the white elm provides when you feel isolated, alone,
misunderstood.
If not the acorn or the elm, the attention diverts to the blackberries
whose high content of vitamins makes you feel prosperous,
abundant and healed from the inner turmoil and emotional
blockages, finding pleasure and joy from each bite.
All gravitational desires pulling you from the water,
And intensity that only the Source has the power to reroute you to
where life is flowing.
Listen for the rumble, babble, and trickles for undistracted direction,
With each sound and step you will find the waterway,
Give thanks,
Relish in the moment,
And take a sip from the spring.
When you do, you will realize the acorn, the elm, and the
blackberries were lessons on your journey, but it is here at the water
you are reborn, renewed, and wooed.
Soul Satisfied.

Prompt: Seeking the True Source of Renewal

In life, many things can distract us from the deeper fulfillment we truly crave—whether it's temporary comforts, distractions, or fleeting joys. Reflect on the journey of being pulled away from what truly nourishes your soul and how you find your way back to the essential source of life and renewal.

Write about the lessons learned from the distractions and how finally drinking from the true well brings lasting satisfaction, rebirth, and peace. How does recognizing and embracing this deeper source change your perspective and your journey?

Casting Call

The location, date and time has been predetermined.
You do not know, but He knows.
Startled by the request for your presence
For a role reflective of the biblical script
And featured on the picture in motion starring you and the rest of
them.
This call does not need bait to lure you
But simply a softly voiced,
"Come, follow me."
The answered call will circle you.

Prompt: Answering the Divine Invitation

Imagine receiving an unexpected call to step into a role greater than
yourself—one that has been planned long before you were aware.
Write about the moment you realize you are being called to a
purpose beyond your own understanding, guided by a quiet,
compelling invitation to follow a higher path. How do you respond
to these summons? What emotions and thoughts arise when you are
invited to participate in a greater story unfolding?

The Journey to Find a Place

This journey, it's not just about joy's embrace,
But shedding the layers, finding our place.
It's seeing through masks, those veils that obscure,
Embracing truths that our hearts endure.

Not about becoming what others prescribe,
But dismantling falsehoods, where truths reside.
It's a path to reveal what's been hidden away,
Seeing through pretense, to our own bright day.

In this journey, it's not just happiness or betterment we seek,
But the crumbling of untruths, making us strong and unique.
So, my dear ones, let's walk this path with grace,
Finding enlightenment in our truth-filled space.

Prompt: The Path to Authenticity

Write about the journey of discovering your true self beyond the
masks and expectations placed on you by others. Explore what it
means to shed falsehoods and embrace your own unique truth, even
when it challenges comfort or superficial happiness. How does
uncovering authenticity reshape your sense of belonging and
purpose? Reflect on the strength that comes from walking this often
difficult but liberating path.

Patience with Power-Filled Process

Through the storms of humility,
Through the trials of rejection,
Through the emotionless waters of isolation,
Through the seasons of dry, unyielding earth
Through the sometimes unbearable, intensive long lasting fires,
Through the winds that sometimes whispered and at times roared
for me to break my connection with The Sacred Source of it all,
I patiently prevailed.
Now, the earthly crops, herbs, bloom with flowering fruits that are
plentiful.
The bathing waters cleansing, with the reassurance of protection,
The fires, though they still come, my reaction to them are much
more peaceful and I let and allow them to transform me and
The airs that whisper sweet nothings in my ear of love filled
worthiness.
And I bask in the elements as they remind, validate, and spiral me in
my purpose to extend grace and mercy in micro and macro doses,
meeting people where they are through acceptance in a sacred shell
of community.
The doors of opportunity open in abundance and all are spiritual
leaders, teachers and guides.
I waited amid the turmoil on the Spirit who made my tribe clear,
distinguishing the fake from the authentic
Such a timely God.
Thank you for everything.

Prompt: Embracing Transformation Through Patience

Write about a challenging journey of growth and transformation that tests your patience through rejection, isolation, and hardship. Explore how staying connected to a sacred source or inner strength helps you endure the storms and fires of life. How does patience shape your understanding of grace, community, and purpose? Reflect on the moment when struggle turns into abundance, and how this process reveals new opportunities and deeper spiritual leadership.

www.ingramcontent.com/pod-product-compliance
Lightning Source LLC
Chambersburg PA
CBHW031002090426
42737CB00008B/643